Ages 4-5

Leap Ahead

Leap Ahead Workbook

English
Home learning made fun

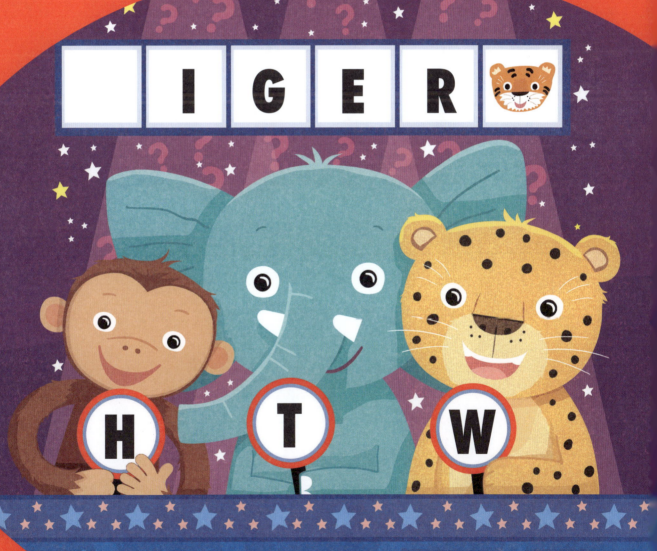

Foundation
English

iglobooks

This is Me!

Draw a picture of yourself:

My name is ....

I am .... years old.

PARENT TIP: It is a big confidence boost for your child if they can write their own name when they start school. Help them find a comfortable pencil grip, then encourage them to copy the letter shapes that make their name.

Rhyming Time

Draw lines to match the rhyming words. Then, find the missing stickers. The first one is done for you.

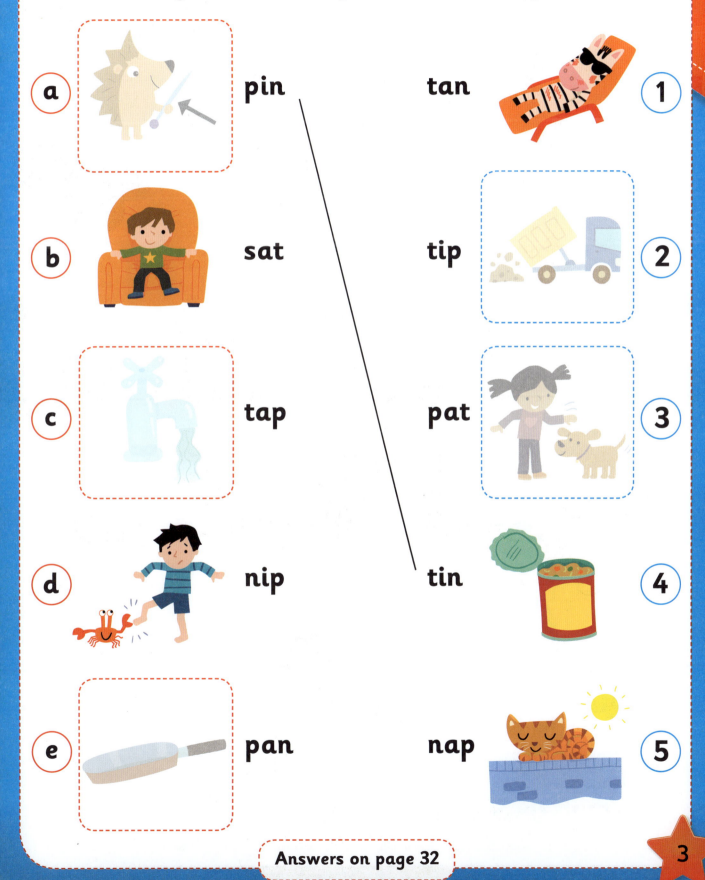

Answers on page 32

Listen and Draw

Listen carefully to a grown-up as they read these instructions. Then, draw a picture of what they describe in the space below.

Instructions:
Put the sun at the top.
Put one tree on each side of the picture.
Give each tree five branches.
Draw a bird in the tree on the right of the picture.
Draw three clouds in the sky.
Put a sheep and a dog on the grass.

4

Word Wheel

Look at each picture around the wheel and say it out loud. Then, look for a sticker that starts with the same sound and put it on the space inside the wheel. The first one is done for you.

Party Letters

Find stickers for the missing balloons and complete the alphabet in time for the party.

PARENT TIP: Sing the alphabet song to help your child learn letter names and remember their order in the alphabet. Try to link letter names to the sound that each letter makes, e.g. "This is letter 's', (pronounced 'es'). It makes an 'sssssss' sound."

What's the First Letter?

Practise writing these letters:

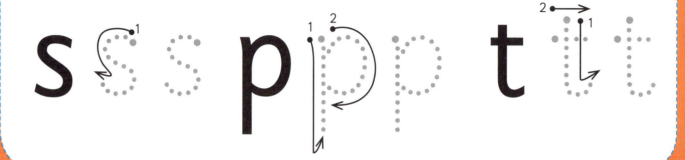

Look at each picture, read the word out loud and choose a letter from the box to fill in the missing first letter. The first one is done for you.

| s | p | t | p | s | p | t |

a) pet
b) ix
c) in
d) en
e) in
f) op
g) ack
h) en

Answers on page 32

Animal Antics

Look at the animals. What do you think they are doing? Find the correct word from the box for each picture.

| act | hop | hit | pat | sit | pick |

a.

b.

c.

d.

e.

f.

Answers on page 32

Zoo I Spy

Play Zoo I Spy in the scene below and take it in turns to ask and answer. How many things can you find beginning with these letters?

a s t p n m d c

Sounds All Around

Say the sound that is above the dot in each word. Then, say the whole word out loud and find the missing stickers.

man    kit    wet

fun    run    win

jog    lap    pig

cot    vet    bag

sad    ham    pet

PARENT TIP: As your child learns to spell, it is important for them to listen for every sound in a word. Encourage them to say each sound separately before blending them together.

What's in the Picture?

Colour in the picture using the code below to reveal a hidden image.

k = 　　　　j = 　　　　r =

l = 　　　　u = 　　　　w =

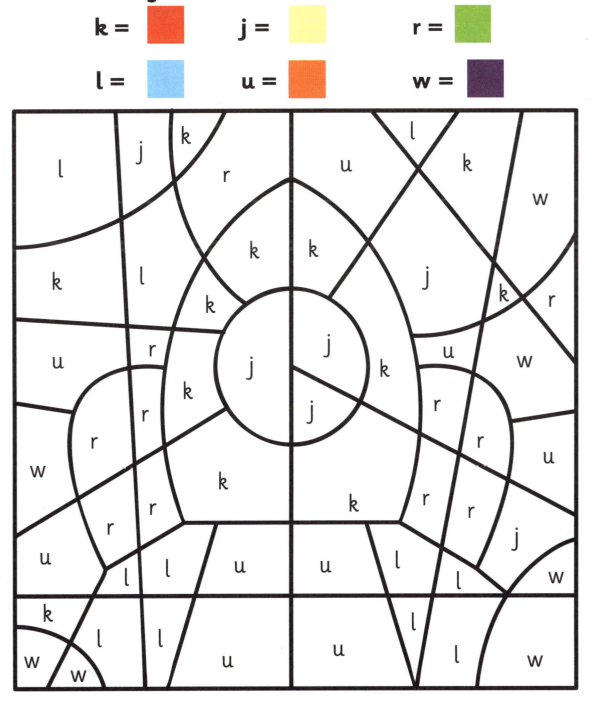

Answers on page 32

PARENT TIP: As well as encouraging pencil control, this activity helps your child to recognise letter shapes and tell them apart from one another.

Mr Mouse's Rocket

Listen to the story. How do you think it should finish? Write your own ending and draw it in the space.

Mr Mouse was hungry. "I need some cheese," he said. He looked in the cupboard, but there was nothing there.

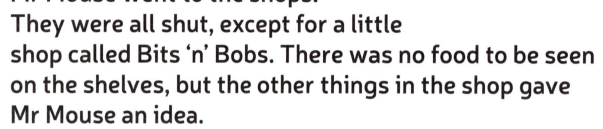

"Where can I find some cheese?" he thought. Mr Mouse went to the shops. They were all shut, except for a little shop called Bits 'n' Bobs. There was no food to be seen on the shelves, but the other things in the shop gave Mr Mouse an idea.

"Could I have some metal, a bag of bolts, one rocket engine, a steering wheel and a small, round window, please?" The shopkeeper came back with a bag of heavy things.

Mr Mouse took the bag home. All night he hammered and fixed and glued and drilled. Every now and then, he looked out the window at the beautiful moon.

Finally, Mr Mouse stopped hammering and looked at what he had made. It was an amazing space rocket! Now he could fly to the moon and bring back all the cheese he would ever want.

He climbed aboard and started the countdown. 10, 9, 8, 7, 6, 5, 4, 3, 2, 1... BLAST OFF!

PARENT TIP: Read the story out loud and ask your child how they want to finish it. Try suggesting a few simple ideas and asking them which one they like best.

Little Words

Read each of the sentences below. Follow the arrows to practise writing each dotted word. Then, write it again at the end of each line.

Jack had a bug.   a a a

He put it in a box,

but the bug got out.

The bug was big.

It went up Mum's leg!

Mum said, "Get it off!"

PARENT TIP: Short words that we use all the time are called 'high-frequency' words. Helping your child to recognise these types of words quickly will make reading much easier for them.

What's in the Picture?

Colour in the picture using the code to reveal a hidden image. What shape can you see?

e = 🟥　　b = 🟩　　f = 🟨

c = 🟦　　a = 🟧　　o = ⬛

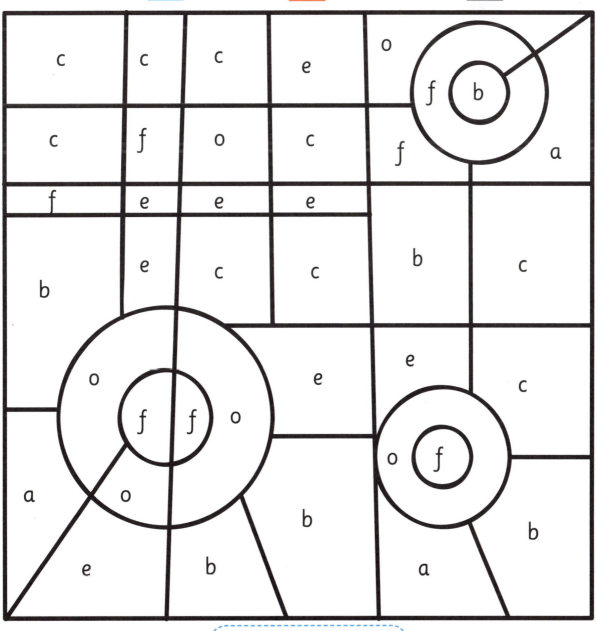

Answers on page 32

PARENT TIP: As well as encouraging pencil control, this activity helps your child to recognise letter shapes and tell them apart from one another.

Cartoon Time

Read the captions under each box and draw pictures to match. Then, tell the story out loud.

1

This is my dad.

2

Today, Dad is ill.

5

At ten, Dad gets up.

6

"I must go out," he says.

3

He is too hot.

4

He has got spots.

7

Then, Mum comes in.

8

"Oh, no!" she cries.
"Go back to bed!"

Missing Letters

Complete the words below using the correct letter from the box. Then, find the stickers to match the words. The first one has been done for you.

| a | o̸ | m | g | e | r | f | d |

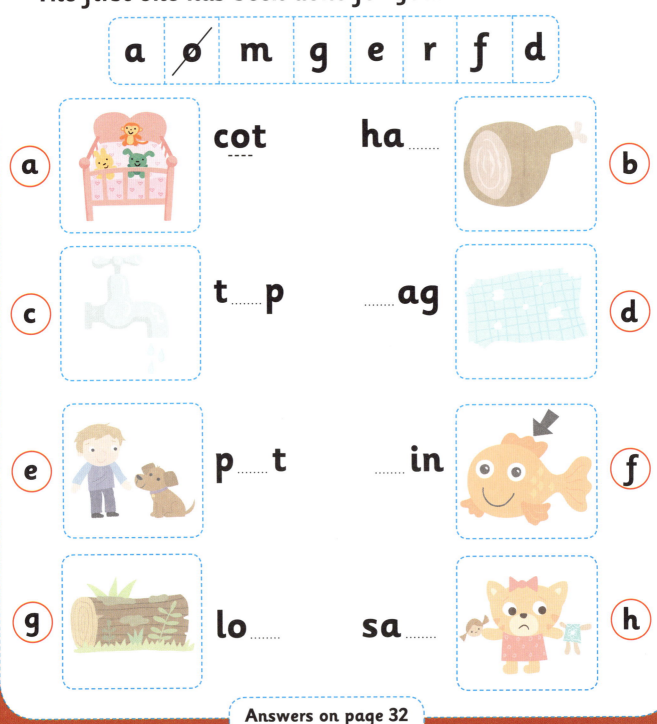

cot   ha__   t__p   __ag   p__t   __in   lo__   sa__

Answers on page 32

PARENT TIP: If your child is not sure of a word, sound-talk the picture first, e.g. 'l-o-g' and then find the letter in the box that makes the missing sound.

Letter Detective

Count the number of times each letter from the box appears in the story. Write the letter by the correct number below. The first one has been done for you. Count the capitals and lower case letters as shown.

| g | M | B | I | i | m | a | r |

It was a dark night when I set off for Tiara Town in search of Mr Big. Mr Big had the diamonds. He had taken them from the museum in a daring robbery. I needed to get them back and give them to the museum.

I checked Mr Big's favourite cafe and his favourite disco, but he wasn't there. I walked around all night, but wherever I went he had been and gone. As the sun began to come up, I went back to my car.

On the windscreen was a note. I picked it up and shook my head when I read it.

Number of Letters	9	31	10	2	17	4	19	10
Letters	I							

Rearrange the letters to spell a clue:

……. ……. …….   ……. …….   ……. ……. …….

Answers on page 32

Word Match

Look at the words on this page and the pictures underneath them. Look for the same word on the opposite page and find the sticker that matches that word. The first three are done for you.

I	go	up	you	we
this	and	at	on	he
she	am	for	see	can
yes	no	it	in	all
get	dog	big	me	mum

get	yes	she	this	I
dog	no	am	and	go
big	it	for	at	up
me	in	see	on	you
mum	all	can	he	we

PARENT TIP: 'High-frequency' words are small words that appear a lot when children are reading. Learning to spot these without sounding them out will speed up your child's reading and make it easier for them, too.

Everyday Words

Read each of these words and copy them in the spaces.

my	....	is	....
look	....	go	....
going	....	the	....
we	....	away	....
she	....	play	....
dog	....	and	....
like	....	look	....
said	....	of	....
was	....	went	....
day	....	come	....

PARENT TIP: If your child is doing well at writing these words, ask them to practise spelling a few from memory. Try having them cover up one word at a time, then writing it so you can check their spelling.

Writing Captions

Look at each of the pictures below. Then, write what you see on the lines underneath. The first one has been done for you.

A pig on the bus.

PARENT TIP: Your child probably won't get each word correct, but encourage them to sound each word before writing it. If some are written correctly, that's a great start!

Come to the Party!

Fill in the missing words on this party invitation.

To ....

Please come to my birthday party!

It is a .... party so please come dressed as a ....

The date for the party is ....

It will start at .... and finish at ....

The address is ....
....
....

I really hope you can come.

From ....

My Dog Pat

Use the pictures as clues to complete the end of each sentence. The first and the last ones are done for you.

My dog is called Pat.

He chases ....

He chews old ....

and sleeps on a ....

Pat loves to ....

and play in the ....

He is lots of fun!

PARENT TIP: To work out each missing word, encourage your child to look at the pictures and try to think of something that rhymes with the previous line.

Supermarket Chaos

Look at the supermarket scene below. Things are in a bit of a mess! Label the scene using the words in the box. The first one is done for you.

tins, fruit, vegetables, till, shop assistant, trolley, basket, customer, frozen food.

My Favourite Things

What are your favourite foods?

....

....

....

....

Draw a picture of your favourite animal:

What is your favourite toy?

....

My best friend's name is ....

Draw a picture of you and your best friend:

Answers

Page 3: Rhyming Time
a – 4, b – 3, c – 5, d – 2, e – 1

Page 6: Party Letters
a, b, c, d, e, f, g, h, i, j, k, l, m,
n, o, p, q, r, s, t, u, v, w, x, y, z.

Page 8: What's the First Letter?
a – pet, b – sit, c – hit, d – hop, e – pick, f – pat

Page 13: What's in the Picture?
A rocket.

Page 17: What's in the Picture?
A tractor.

Page 20: Missing Letters
a – cot, b – ham, c – tap, d – rag, e – pet, f – fin,
g – log, h – sad

Page 21: Letter Detective
Clue: I am Mr Big

Page 28: Supermarket Chaos
a – tins, b – frozen food, c – vegetables, d – fruit, e – shop assistant, f – trolley, g – customer, h – basket, i – till

page 3

page 5

page 6

cehijlnoqtvxy

page 12

page 20

page 22